D1437243

TO SET BEFORE
A QUEEN

TO SET BEFORE A QUEEN

by

MRS. McKEE

formerly cook to
Her Majesty The Queen
and Her Majesty The Queen Mother

London
ARLINGTON BOOKS

TO SET BEFORE A QUEEN
first published 1963 by
Arlington Books London
with Constable and Company
printed by Hely Thom Ltd. of Dublin

© *Alma McKee 1963*

CONTENTS

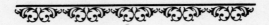

INTRODUCTION

INTRODUCTION

How strange it is to look back over forty years and realize that you have devoted most of your life to food.

Yet cooking is a large part of most women's lives. To some it is a chore and to others it brings pleasure. I enjoyed cooking when a child in Sweden because, on a simple level, I had found that here was a way to please people and make them happy.

I leave it to others to rhapsodize about the *art* of cooking. To me it is an expression of love and care. I think most women will know what I mean.

Male chefs in the great houses I have known produce masterpieces of haute cuisine. Magnificent in every way. If you do not happen to like a particular dish, then it is your bad taste—but that is not really the point. Is it, or is it not, a masterpiece, they query anxiously? Whether or not you actually like it, is another matter.

This I think is the essential difference between the male and female approach to cooking. A man cooks with his head, a woman with her heart.

When I first went to cook for Princess Elizabeth at Clarence House in 1951, I was told that I was the only female chef in charge of a royal kitchen. I had previously cooked for King Peter of Yugoslavia and his wife, but that was different. They were very young at the time when I was there, and very informal.

Like most Swedes, I was horribly shy, and on that first day at Clarence House, extremely nervous. I knew deep down that I could manage the job and that hundreds, if not thousands of people had enjoyed my food. But occasionally you might meet someone who does not happen to like your sort of food. There is nothing you can really do about it. Everybody has their own style of cooking. And at fifty-five it was too late to change mine. I prayed I wouldn't have to try.

With my first meal came the first royal compliment. It was to be the forerunner of many, for Her Majesty is one of the most appreciative people I have ever worked for; frequently sending messages of congratulation or thanking me personally after a special dinner. There is something quite riveting about her smile, and I can assure you that when that smile is levelled at you personally, there is nothing you would not do for her.

Perhaps because Her Majesty is such a very inspiring person, I felt that my cooking was at its best during these carefree days at Clarence House. I had never opened a recipe book, and I cooked as always by taste, adjusting the flavour and adding to the dish as I went along. The ideas flowed and I ceased to worry that perhaps in one day I would be cooking lunch for four Queens, followed by a dinner party at which every guest was royal.

It would be naive to imagine that royalty always dine off rare delicacies, though people are sometimes surprised when I go to the trouble of describing how to cook a good kipper or haddock which the royal family certainly enjoy. Perhaps it is because the royal family, of all people, have no need to impress that everything is judged on merit alone. In my time at Clarence House, stuffed cabbage received as much appreciation as pheasant or grouse. More, in fact, as they were always overflowing with game from the estates at Balmoral and Sandringham.

When I first came over from Sweden between the wars and married a Scotsman, people were still eating seven course meals in the grander houses. Now it is only on rare occasions that the Royal family have five courses. Usually it is not more than three, and the food is good, but simple.

When the King died and Her Majesty eventually moved to Buckingham Palace, I stayed behind to cook for the Queen Mother and Princess Margaret. Before leaving, the Queen asked me to write down a selection of my recipes.

As I was not accustomed to making notes of exact weights and measurements nor to describing my method of cooking in English (I still wrote in Swedish), the notes I wrote must have been decidedly sketchy. In fact I felt sorry for the chef whose job it would be to decipher them.

When Her Majesty reads this book, I would like to offer my profoundest apologies.

For a time at Clarence House I was flattered to find that my name as a chef was getting known. By this I mean that it was known to the small circle of top calibre chefs who are employed by the few remaining large private households, or who work for clubs and distinguished restaurants. These chefs, all men, invited me to dinner and in turn gave me their masterpieces, generously telling me the recipes. Or some of them. I asked them back and gave of my best. It was all very jolly until they asked me for my 'secrets'. Sooner than reveal that I had only the vaguest idea of how much of this or that I put into a dish, I had to preserve a mysterious silence.

This was the end of the dinner parties.

After this, and the inadequate recipes I was forced to give to the Queen, I started studying myself at work as it were; and for the first time started weighing things and analysing my methods.

All my life people have asked me for recipes and I have suffered from the fact that my inability to reveal the details has been interpreted as professional secrecy.

The recipes in this book, though only a fraction of the dishes I have cooked in a lifetime, are some of the ones I have been asked for most often, and I am happy that I can at last supply them. I must, at this point, thank Miss Maureen Owen for all her help in preparing them for the press.

I am happy too for the opportunity of setting out a few of the true principles of Swedish cookery—a sadly unknown branch of gastronomy.

Swedes like their food. We like our food to be good and we like our food to be well cooked. Above all we like to be able to taste the *flavour* of that good meat, or fish, or whatever it is we are cooking. You will not find us flinging a glass of sherry or wine into a stew in the vague hope of making it more interesting.

Instead our cookery is based on scientific principles more concerned with drawing out the flavour of the basic ingredient than obscuring it.

But perhaps the best advice I can give, for anyone who wants to make other people happy with their food, is to cook with love and trust your palate.

Taste the food as you go along and do not be afraid to adjust the flavour according to your palate. Due to the temperature, season and type of storage; food is susceptible to a hundred and one variations.

As for love—no dish should be served without it.

SAUCES

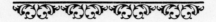

SAUCES

The English have over two dozen religions, but only one sauce, I was told when I first came to this country.

This is the most wonderful sauce for everyone and is served with fish, chicken, vegetables and with any meat that might be dull on its own.

The ingredients are:

6 oz of fresh butter; 4 oz flour; ½ pint of milk; ½ teaspoon of salt; a pinch of grated nutmeg, pepper and sugar.

Melt half the quantity of butter in a saucepan, stir in the flour, add the milk, or if preferred a little cream and water, stir continuously over a low heat until thick and smooth. Add some more milk if necessary, then the seasoning, sugar and nutmeg. Let the sauce simmer gently for two minutes then remove from heat, stir in the rest of the cold butter in small lumps until well mixed.

This is the White Sauce. The basic King of sauces which lends triumph and lustre to plain foods when smooth and creamy; but leads to depression and indigestion when greasy and lumpy. A simple sauce, a simple method, but greasy and lumpy it will most likely be if you do not remove that saucepan from the heat and add the remainder of the butter last of all.

I am a great admirer of the English White sauce, and use masses of it myself. But rarely, I admit, as a means to an end in itself, instead I use it as the foolproof basis to a good many other sauces and dishes.

There is only one way to make a good sauce, and that is with love and care, which is why you cannot knock up a quick meal in a hurry and hope to put matters right by disguising indifferent food with a highly flavoured sauce.

Out of all the members of the royal family, the Queen Mother was perhaps the most appreciative of a good sauce, frequently sending messages of thanks and mentioning the sauce by name.

When I returned to Clarence House to cook for the Queen Mother after Princess Elizabeth became Queen and moved to Buckingham Palace, I was extremely nervous, since the Queen Mother had always been accustomed to a male chef, I was taken on under a temporary basis to see how we got along together. This was a point of view I perfectly understood as in England all the really big kitchens are run by men and the administrative work of a large kitchen with a big staff is probably better done by a man. For although the Queen and her family numbered more than her mother and sister; the Queen Mother and Princess Margaret had a larger staff, most of whom had to be cooked for by me. Also the Queen Mother and Princess Margaret frequently entertained separately, sometimes on the same day. If the Queen Mother was doubtful, I was certainly extremely apprehensive, and at the last moment before she arrived at the newly decorated Clarence House I discovered that in the chaos of the move between the two households, there were only two saucepans in the house. I had hardly met my new employer and my mind was blank of everything except where to find essential tools.

The Coronation was imminent and although the harassed Comptroller had not yet issued the Programme, there was certain to be a huge amount of entertaining.

Into my mind came the soothing proportions of

CUMBERLAND SAUCE

3 tablespoons red currant jelly
1 tablespoon orange marmalade (the thick kind)
juice of half a lemon

1 wineglass sherry
pinch of cayenne pepper
½ teaspoon dry English mustard mixed in water

Mix the ingredients together roughly and serve with cold ham, game, smoked veal and hot or cold duck.

I do not remember with which meat I served this classic sauce, but it was a fortunate choice. The Queen Mother told me that she had not eaten this sauce since before the war and had almost despaired of finding it again. Cumberland sauce, is of course simple to make but the proportions are all-important.

Rapport having been established with the Queen Mother, I went on to find other sauces that appealed to her.

Italian Sauce served with pasta is popular with all the royal family. And if there was a choice of several dishes to be selected by royalty for the following day's menu this one usually won . . .

One slice of beef; 1 large onion; 1 glass red wine; tablespoon of tomato extract; 1 carrot; 1 piece of celery; 1 oz butter; 1 tablespoon of nut oil; bouquet of parsley, thyme and bay leaf; pepper and salt and 2 glasses of water; 1 cup of grated parmesan cheese.

Dice beef and onion. Place butter and oil to heat in a saucepan. When hot throw in beef and onion and brown.

2

Add wine and allow the liquid to boil and reduce then add the tomato extract, carrot and celery, the herbs, pepper and salt and the water. Cover and simmer for about two hours. When cooked, strain the gravy, chop the meat and absorb it into the sauce. Add nearly all the grated parmesan cheese and pour the sauce over pasta (if spaghetti is used, it should not have boiled for more than twenty minutes). Finish by sprinkling cheese over the top and serve very hot.

Boiled chicken and steamed fish are two things frequently fated to meet with White sauce. Here are two sauces, white in appearance, but more interesting in flavour than the traditional béchamel.

SAUCE ALLEMANDE

1½ ozs butter
1 oz flour
2 yolks of eggs
1 tablespoon of cream
1 teaspoon lemon juice

1¼ pints of chicken or fish stock
pinch of nutmeg
salt and pepper
pinch of sugar

Melt butter in pan and add the flour, stir for a few minutes without allowing it to brown. Dilute with rather more than a pint of stock and stir until it boils. Season with pepper, salt and sugar and nutmeg and simmer for ten minutes. Mix yolks of eggs, cream and butter together in a separate basin and add to hot sauce after taking it off the heat.

SAUCE TARRAGON [for fish]

½ lb butter.
1 tablespoon dry tarragon leaves
½ tablespoon of tarragon vinegar

the juice of half a lemon
pinch each of salt, cayenne, pepper, sugar

This is a cold sauce and requires no cooking.

Cream the butter in a basin and gradually work in the vinegar and lemon juice. Stirring all the time add the tarragon leaves, pepper and salt and small pinch of sugar. The texture should be light and creamy. Serve with all fish, particularly recommended for deep fried dover sole. For looks try warming two tablespoons in hot water and scooping out the mixture so that it resembles a pile of heaped up eggs in the sauceboat.

Mayonnaise is a lot more to me than just a coating for cold food. It can and should be, varied in flavour to suit the dish with which it is served and it also serves as a basis for many other sauces and dishes. Mayonnaise can be thickened for sandwiches and canapés and piped for decoration. Altogether, a most versatile sauce but one that cannot be hurried.

4 *yolks of eggs;* 1 *tablespoon vinegar;* 1½ *pints nut oil or olive oil (I prefer the former);* ½ *teaspoon salt; juice of half a lemon; dash of cayenne pepper;* ½ *teaspoon dry mustard mixed with water; pinch sugar;* 2 *tablespoons hot water.*

Essential—a good whisk. I have a Swedish one made of birch branches which looks like a little brush.

Mix egg yolks, salt and mustard into a paste. Then start dripping in the oil whisking all the time and gradually absorbing the vinegar. Use the hot water, a little at a time in order to thin the mixture. Continue like this, alternately softening and stiffening the mixture for about twenty minutes. The lemon juice should alternate with the vinegar and hot water as a softening agent. Finish off by adding the seasoning and sugar and drop the last spoonful of hot water into the side of the bowl.

In all, the operation will have taken at least half an hour, but this recipe will give you a good quantity of mayonnaise, which if bottled will keep for up to three months, and can be used as a basis for a sauce or, thickened with chopped hard boiled eggs—as a sandwich filling.

Some people go to extremes about the temperature of the room when making mayonnaise, but so long as you are not standing over a hot stove or operating in sub zero conditions there is no need to worry. It is important though to see that all the ingredients are at the same temperature before you start.

All cooks need to have short cuts to resort to in times of crises. My hectic days came about when the Queen Mother and Princess Margaret were living at Clarence House and frequently gave separate dinner parties with only an hour's interval between them.

The food, of course, was always different. I don't think I ever used the same menu twice during the whole of my time at Clarence House. All the same I often had reason to be grateful to my bottled mayonnaise. The following are two entirely different sauces made on a basis of this useful mixture, and I used to look upon them as life savers.

TARTARE SAUCE

½ *pint mayonnaise*
¼ *pint whipped cream*
2 *slices onion*
finely chopped half dessert
   apple, cored and peeled

1 *dessertspoon roughly chopped*
   capers, bottled in vinegar
juice of half a lemon
½ *teaspoon English mustard*
   mixed with a little water
½ *teaspoon castor sugar*

Mix all the ingredients together in a bowl without cooking and serve with deep fried fish or shellfish.

LEMON SAUCE

$\frac{3}{4}$ *pint mayonnaise*　　　　*half teaspoon paste mustard*
$\frac{1}{2}$ *pint cream*　　　　　　　*pinch of sugar*
juice of half a lemon

Whip cream, stir in mayonnaise, gradually add mustard, sugar and lemon juice and serve cold with any fish that comes to mind.

This is another simple sauce, which, according to the royal family, can't be improved upon. At any rate they all ate masses of it.

HORSERADISH

Make $\frac{1}{2}$ pint of white sauce substituting beef stock for milk, and while hot add a tablespoon of grated horseradish. If fresh horseradish is not available use double the quantity of bottled horseradish but be careful to use a kind which is not too vinegary.

Serve with hot brisket of beef.

Hidden in among the sauces—a confession.

I frequently used garlic when cooking for royalty.

Apart from being told to curtsey whenever I saw Her Royal Highness and to avoid the use of garlic, nobody told me how to behave or what to cook when I first joined the present Queen and her husband at Clarence House in 1951.

This aversion for garlic, also shared by Princess Margaret, though not the other members of the royal family, seemed understandable enough for obvious reasons and to start with I kept to instructions. One day, however, I 'forgot'. No complaints followed, in fact there were compliments and thereafter I continued to use traces of garlic in cooking undetected. In my opinion you never should be able to detect an overpowering flavour of garlic in any dish, and the cloves, if used whole should always be removed before serving. The only time I ever saw a dish sent back with complaints from royalty was when an unfortunate chef once overdid the garlic and sent the result to table with the cloves still in it.

'We *never* eat garlic' came the message. Well . . .

The following was a favourite at Clarence House and I can also remember serving it with Sunday lunch at Royal Lodge Windsor:

PIMENTO AND TOMATO PROVENÇALE

a tablespoon each of butter and olive or nut oil

1 pimento, seeded and quartered

½ lb tomatoes skinned and quartered

1 clove of garlic

Heat butter and oil together in saucepan and drop in one clove of garlic. Add pimento and tomato and simmer for twenty-five minutes. Put through sieve or mixer and serve with hot roast meat.

This is a sauce which is particularly good with all meat, fish or game which is inclined to be on the dry side.

RÉMOULADE

4 hard boiled eggs

3 yolks of eggs

4 anchovies

1 tablespoon capers

1 tablespoon French or English mustard paste

¼ pint olive oil

¼ pint tarragon vinegar

½ pint whipped cream

Put the yolks of hardboiled eggs through a sieve, stir in

raw yolks and mix to a smooth paste. Add the oil and vinegar gradually while mixing, then the mustard, capers and anchovies. Lastly, stir in the whipped cream. No cooking.

BROWN BUTTER SAUCE

6 *ozs butter*   1 *wineglass tarragon vinegar*
½ *teaspoon black pepper*

Brown the butter gently over a slow heat taking care not to let it burn. Let the butter cool and put it through a fine sieve. Boil the vinegar and pepper in separate saucepan until reduced to half the quantity and stir in the butter gradually. During the making of this sauce, the pan should stand in a bain marie and great care must be taken to see that the mixture does not boil.

Serve with hot braised cutlets or fried fish.

TOMATO SAUCE

1 *oz of butter*   1 *clove of garlic*
1 *chopped onion*   *water to cover*
6 *sliced tomatoes*   *light seasoning*
2 *cloves*

Put all the ingredients in a saucepan and cover with water. Bring to the boil, lower heat and simmer for fifteen minutes. Strain and serve with lamb cutlets, steak, pasta, pork, etc.

The next sauce is a life saver. I first created it as a substitute for the wearying processes of Hollandaise sauce. Many people mistake it for Hollandaise, yet it has grown to be a favourite. And when served with hot poached salmon, Dover sole or lemon sole, or with cold asparagus it makes a delicious dish.

SAUCE CITRON

3 *yolks of eggs*
½ *pint of single cream*
juice of ½ *a lemon*
½ *teaspoon of salt*

½ *teaspoon of sugar*
1 *wineglass of fish stock if
   being used with fish*
2 *tablespoons of butter*

Mix the cream, egg yolks and stock in a saucepan. Heat. Whisk until a custard-like consistency is reached but do not allow to boil. When frothy add the slightly softened butter a little at a time. Finish by adding the lemon juice, salt and sugar.

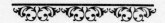

SWEDISH
COOKING

SWEDISH COOKING

I would like to say something about the Swedes. Hardly anybody ever does. Honestly now, apart from Dag Hammarskjöld, some nice furniture and prohibition, how much do you hear about Sweden and the Swedes?

To their great disadvantage with the rest of the world, the Swedes are two things:

They are shy. And they are poor publicity men.

Their shyness earns them the reputation of being off-hand and difficult. That song 'Wonderful, Wonderful Copenhagen' got a lot of Swedes down, because although Stockholm is equally wonderful none of them would think of saying so, far less, singing about it.

Sweden has many brilliant artists, scientists, designers and men of commerce but somehow they lack the knack of telling other people about their achievements.

For instance, how many people talk about Swedish cooking in the same way as they talk about French, Italian, Chinese or Spanish cooking?

Yet there is such a thing as Swedish cooking, but instead of people knowing it for what it is—very good and distinctly savoury—various aspects of Swedish cookery have been gradually absorbed into modern cookery principles without anyone knowing where they came from.

Swedish cookery is scientifically based on health principles, but as well as that we like our dishes to be well flavoured. I have noticed recently that many recipes for meat and savoury food include a pinch of sugar. This is typically Swedish. For many generations Swedes have known the value of sugar in bringing out a savoury flavour. We also use other sweetening aids which are not apparent in the final result, like red currant jelly, or treacle.

People talk about the salt of the earth, but for hundreds of years, Swedes have known the value of its sugar too, and it is only just recently that other people have caught on as well.

I suppose you could say that my own cooking is a mixture of Swedish and English cooking. I have a great admiration for good English cooking. I can think of nothing better than the British method of roasting meat, it is something that other nations admire and envy and seem incapable of imitating. I know this because frequently, when abroad I have been called upon in desperation by hungry British expatriates to produce that simple favourite—so difficult to the Continental mind— roast beef.

The British royal family prefer all that is best in English cooking as a staple diet, but have an open mind on food and like trying new dishes always provided they are good of their kind.

As the royal family ate a lot of game, I often used Swedish cookery principles to provide variety. Since although roast game is a luxury to most people it can become as boring as baked beans if served with constant repetition.

Despite all the grouse and pheasant on hand at Balmoral, Prince Philip's favourite dish was the humble pigeon. I remember him coming round to my kitchen window at Birk-hall one morning and asking what there was for dinner. When I told him it was to be grouse, he at once went out with his gun and returned with a bag of pigeons which I casseroled according to the following recipe.

SWEDISH PIGEONS

four wood pigeons	*seasoning*
tablespoon nut oil	*½ pint cream*
tablespoon butter	*2 tablespoons flour*
half a pint of stock or water	*2 ozs butter*
* with Bovril*	*(serves six)*
1 tablespoon red currant jelly	

Clean pigeons well and dry thoroughly. Braise in a saucepan with the butter and oil until brown. When well browned add half a pint of stock and season well. Cover and simmer for an hour and a half. Allow to cool, then cut each pigeon in half pulling out as many small bones as possible. Place in a warm casserole dish, cover and keep hot. Make a stock from the pigeon bones and simmer for an hour. Then strain gravy from bones into another saucepan.

For the sauce: Mix two tablespoons flour with water, add to the gravy, stirring over a low heat for five minutes. Add the red currant jelly, two tablespoons of butter, pepper and salt—and just before serving—the cream. Pour a little of the sauce over the pigeons and serve the rest separately.

Serve with plain potatoes, peas and cranberry sauce.

This recipe is suitable for game of any kind.

BRAISED FILLET OF BEEF

2 lbs of beef from the undercut	*1 parsnip*
¼ lb larding bacon	*1 carrot*
1 tablespoon nut oil	*1 onion*
½ teacup single cream	*2 sprigs parsley*
1 oz butter	*3 anchovies*
1 wineglass sweet sherry	*bay leaf*
2 tablespoons flour	*pepper and salt*
½ pint water or stock	

Tie larding bacon round fillets and turn in a saucepan with the oil and butter until brown. Remove from pan. Chop the onion, carrot, parsnip and parsley and brown in the saucepan with the bay leaf. Add one cup of water. Season with pepper and salt and add the anchovies. Replace the meat on top of the vegetables and braise gently for an hour. Remove the meat and vegetables and take the string and bacon from the beef. Keeping the meat in a low oven, reduce the gravy by boiling for ten minutes. Add the sherry and two tablespoons of flour and boil until the fat separates. Skim off the fat. Add more stock and stir making a smooth sauce. Strain, check seasoning. Serve the meat with the sauce and accompanied by small boiled potatoes and carrots glazed with butter.

Prince Charles was a little boy of about four when I was at Clarence House, and Princess Anne a tiny porcelain skinned baby. As I used to work in a clean white overall everyday, Prince Charles called me the lady in white. A nickname that subsequently caught on with the press.

I do not believe in nursery meals being dull, but often with children, they get a craze on something and you have to keep repeating it until you can interest them in something else.

With Prince Charles it was meat balls made from chicken or veal, though quite often in those days it was made from rabbit as well. At that time Prince Charles loved using the house telephone, much to the confusion of the office staff, and he would frequently call me in the kitchen and ask for meat balls.

Actually these meat balls are dignified under the name of Frikadellar in Sweden where they are a classic dish and used in a variety of ways. Frikadellar floated on a dish of clear consommé for instance can be a smart dinner party first course.

FRIKADELLAR

½ lb raw chicken
½ lb raw veal
3 tablespoons breadcrumbs
3 eggs
2 tablespoons salt
a teaspoon castor sugar

½ teaspoon pepper
½ to ¾ pint single cream
juice of half a lemon
2 pints chicken or veal stock
1 tablespoon flour

Put meat through mincer three times. Soften breadcrumbs with a little cream and add to meat. Stirring all the time add some more cream and two eggs. Season with salt and pepper. Roll into balls or sausage shapes. Drop into stock and boil for fifteen minutes. The stock need not cover the frikadellars.

Just before serving make the following sauce with the stock:

Mix flour to a thin paste with water, add to the stock together with the rest of the cream, one yolk of egg, lemon juice and the sugar.

Pour this sauce over the frikadellar and serve hot with creamed potatoes or rice and spinach.

In Sweden we also use frikadellar as an excellent addition to a cold buffet, or as a stuffing for chicken. And you can steam it as a paté decorated with truffles and olives and set in aspic.

Any housewife who has ever been caught with a last minute party will have some idea of how I felt when one fine morning at Clarence House I was told that there was to be a party for forty-five royal guests that same evening. Added to that, there was nothing in the house as we had expected royalty to be out that evening, and on looking round, I found that we had no really big dishes.

The first thing I did was to borrow some enormous dishes from Buckingham Palace, rather like a young housewife borrowing from her mother in an emergency. The next problem was to think of something to put on them.

Everyone in the kitchen stared at me blankly.

'I'm sure you will manage beautifully Mrs. McKee' said the Comptroller serenely. 'If it will help, I can arrange for you to have a car and chauffeur for any shopping you may need.'

I jumped smartly into the car, directed the chauffeur towards Soho, and put in some fast thinking on the way.

As usual I had to visualise the finished table in detail before I could start planning. As a matter of fact I rather enjoy the stimulation of preparing a party. It is the dull every-day chores that clog the imagination.

On this occasion my centrepiece was:

SWEDISH GAMMON

a gammon weighing about 8 lbs	Piece of cinnamon stick
½ lb black treacle	ground cinnamon
2 pints pineapple juice	demerera sugar
4 cloves	dry mustard

Soak gammon for 24 hours if possible. Wash and place in a large saucepan, three quarters filled with cold water. Bring to the boil and remove scum. Add the black treacle, cloves, pineapple juice and cinnamon stick. Boil for four hours. Allow to cool in its own juice and when cold pull off the skin. Rub dry mustard all over the fat and make a mixture of a dessertspoon of ground cinnamon and demerera sugar and spread on top. Place in a very hot oven to brown quickly. Remove when golden brown. Can be served hot or cold.

BRAISED VEAL IN THE SWEDISH MANNER

2 *lbs of leg of veal*	2 *sprigs parsley*
2 *ozs butter*	1 *clove of garlic*
1 *carrot*	½ *pint veal stock*
1 *large onion*	*seasoning*

Tie up the boned veal with string and braise in butter until brown. Add the veal stock, sliced carrot and onion and 2 sprigs parsley and the clove of garlic. Season well cover the pan and cook slowly for one and a half hours. When cooked remove meat and untie the string. Remove the vegetables and reduce the gravy by boiling for ten minutes. Glaze the meat with a little of the gravy and keep hot.

Make the sauce from the following ingredients:

1 *tablespoon flour; 2 cups milk; 2 tablespoons cream; 1 tablespoon red currant jelly.*

Dilute the flour in the milk and add to the boiling veal gravy, stirring well. When thickened, strain the gravy into a small saucepan and add the red currant jelly. When well absorbed, stir in the cream. Serve separately.

An accompaniment of lettuce and cucumber salad with a vinegar dressing and small boiled potatoes braised in butter is recommended.

ROASTED DUCK

1 *duck*	2 *cloves*
2 *dessert apples*	½ *cup salt*
1 *duck liver*	1 *lb prunes*
1 *glass claret*	*seasoning*

Soak the prunes overnight in cold water. Core and quarter the apples and insert the cloves. Clean the duck in hot water containing the salt, then rinse inside and out in cold water and drain on a towel for ten minutes. Season duck with salt and pepper inside and out and stuff with the apples and half a pound of prunes. Stone the other half pound of prunes and put in a saucepan with water and let them boil until soft. Remove then place in another saucepan with a little of the prune juice and a pinch of salt and keep simmering on a low heat. Truss the duck and rub the breast with salt and pepper and the duck's liver. Place it in a roasting pan and cover the breast with buttered greaseproof paper. Roast in a hot oven for one hour and twenty minutes. Lower the heat after half an hour and baste in its own juice. When the duck is cooked remove it from the oven, place on a dish and keep warm. Skim fat from the gravy.

To make the sauce you will need:

1 *tablespoon flour*; ½ *pint stock* (*preferably beef*); ½ *cup prune juice*; 1 *dessertspoon orange marmalade*; 1 *glass claret*; 1 *tablespoon duck fat*.

Using the skimmed gravy from the duck add the flour and some stock and, stirring well, make the sauce. Allow to simmer for ten minutes and strain into a small saucepan. Add some prune juice, ½ glass of claret and the orange marmalade. Season if necessary, strain the gravy and keep hot. Put the tablespoon of duck fat on the stoned prunes in the saucepan and a little claret and let it simmer for a few minutes reducing to a glaze. Serve as garnish to the duck.

Excellent with red cabbage and new potatoes.

Perhaps after trying some of these Swedish recipes you will understand the principle behind Swedish cookery; the sweetening agents used in the recipes do not intrude on the final flavour but serve to bring out the savoury aspect of the dish. Gravy is always reduced to preserve the essential juices and concentrate the flavour.

I hope you will enjoy Swedish cooking and the next time you see sugar in a savoury recipe perhaps you will remember where the idea first came from!

SPECIAL DISHES

SPECIAL DISHES

From my days at Clarence House a few dishes spring to mind that were special in a certain way. They are not necessarily grand dishes, though some are; others were made from very humble ingredients indeed, but I remember them chiefly for the pleasure they gave.

The following dish, for instance, I have cooked for more crowned and uncrowned heads than I can remember. On leaving Lord Rothermere his last words were a request for this recipe. The ingredients could hardly be more prosaic.

I will not strain my French, but merely call it plain . . .

STUFFED CABBAGE

1 *large white cabbage*
1 *lb of good sausages (skinned)*
butter for frying
½ *pint of seasoned stock*
½ *pint of good gravy*
1 *cup of milk*

Cut out the stalk of the cabbage and parboil in salted water for five minutes. Remove, drain cabbage, separate the leaves and cut away the hard centre and veins. The sausage meat should be taken from good quality pork sausages as sausage meat sold by the pound is seldom as satisfactory. Mix the sausagemeat with milk to soften. Place a tablespoon of sausagemeat on each cabbage leaf and fold round. It should not be necessary to tie up the leaves with cotton. Fry the stuffed leaves in butter, basting all the time until brown all over. Place the rolls in a flat bottomed fireproof dish and keep warm. Then pour some stock into the frying pan in which the cabbage has been browned, stir and strain over the cabbage leaves. Add half a pint of thickened gravy and a knob of butter, cover the dish and simmer for twenty minutes. Dish up by boiling down the gravy a little and pouring over the cabbage.

Now that more turkeys are consumed, and at times other than just Christmas, people will perhaps be looking for new ways of preparing this admirable bird, so useful for serving large numbers of people.

There is a family feeling about roast turkey. It looks as good as it tastes, its very appearance speaks of good cheer.

I did the following recipe several times at Clarence House, both hot and cold. Although the preparation is somewhat of a fiddle; its satisfying appearance as the centrepiece of a party table, plus the delightful secret of its contents—makes the effort worthwhile.

DINDON FARCIE RÔTI

a plump turkey weighing around 12 lbs
filling:
   1 lb gammon
   1 lb of veal or chicken
½ pint of cream
2 tablespoons of bread-crumbs softened in a little warm milk
seasoning
oil

Clean the bird. Cut open from the backbone and carefully free the turkey of all bones except a small knob at the end of each leg. Leave the wings intact. Flatten the bird and stuff it with the chicken cream mixture (method on page 85). Carefully stretch back the skin and sew up the bird to resemble its original shape. Truss as usual, pushing the wings up and tying back the legs. Rub some oil well into the turkey so that it remains moist. Start in a hot oven, reduce the heat after half an hour and roast for a further two and a half hours. Baste once or twice but do not move the bird while cooking.

To serve cold: baste with a little reduced gravy while cooling to make a glaze. When cold right through, slice thinly right across the bird and put together again.

I take no credit for the next recipe. It was sent to me by Government House, Africa where members of the royal family had enjoyed this speciality. Probably, because it comes from Africa, I always think of serving it on a warm summer's evening. I think too, of a gold and white dining room in London, fragrant with flowers and a young Princess not yet weighed down with the responsibilities of Queenship, entertaining her friends.

AFRICAN SOUFFLÉ

8 *hardboiled eggs*
8 *ozs of stiff mayonnaise*
1 *pint of warm aspic jelly*
4 *whites of eggs*
¼ *oz of gelatine*

1 *truffle*
teaspoon each of Harvey's,
    Worcester and Anchovy
    sauce
salt and pepper

Cut the truffle in half, slice one half for decoration and chop the other half finely. Slice two eggs and keep for decorating the top of the souffle. Pass the other egg yolks through a sieve. Add the soaked gelatine to half of the warm aspic and cool slightly. Add seasoning, and prepared sauces, sieved egg yolks and chopped truffle to the mayonnaise. Whip the whites of eggs and when firm add the reinforced aspic. Mix all together and pour into a prepared soufflé dish. Allow to set, then decorate with the sliced eggs and truffle and coat with the other half pint of aspic.

When I first went to Clarence House, Princess Elizabeth was the wife of a Naval Officer. Prince Philip's ship was in Malta at the time, and the Princess eagerly looked forward to their reunions. At times, in that happy household it was just like being with any well appointed, fairly well-to-do family. The routine ran smoothly, the domestic climate was calm. And there wasn't the same atmosphere among the staff which I learned to recognize later, of competition for royal favour when even a smile would be analyzed and talked about for days. So natural and informal was the atmosphere, that often for weeks on end one would forget that this was a royal household watched by the eyes of the world.

True, whenever Prince Charles went out people waved to him and he would sometimes ask why. But the little boy took this to be a general manifestation of goodwill and waved back as part of the game.

But even in those early days, the Princess's private life was never entirely her own. Prince Philip had been on his ship for some time when the Princess planned a visit to Malta. Preparations were going happily ahead when suddenly one of the newspapers launched an attack on the Princess for enjoying herself abroad.

This criticism, unfair and absurd as it was, came as a bombshell to everyone at Clarence House, and somehow cast a cloud over the preparations. The Princess went to Malta just the same; and as she departed the staff at Clarence House gave her a special send off.

I heard that during his stay in Malta Prince Philip had

developed a liking for Cannelloni made in the local fashion, and I obtained the recipe.

Somehow, however, I never cared to make the dish while at Clarence House. I have tried it since, though, and it is a good recipe.

CANNELLONI

paste:
1¾ *lbs of flour*
4 *eggs*

1 *teaspoon of salt*
4 *tablespoons of oil*
¾ *of a pint of warm water*

Place the flour on the table making a well and break the eggs into the middle. Add the salt and oil. Add the water and mix without working the paste too much. Cover with a serviette to prevent the paste forming a crust and leave for about half an hour. Then roll out fairly thin and cut rectangles, approximately three inches by two and a half. Put in slightly salted water and cook from seven to eight minutes. Drain and put in basin of cold water. Take them out and place on a damp cloth.

sauce: 2 *lbs of beef or veal;* 2 *large chopped onions; one glass of white wine;* 2 *or* 3 *chopped tomatoes;* 1 *tablespoon of flour;* ½ *cup of stock, salt, pepper, thyme, bay leaf and parsley; lard for cooking;* ½ *lb of finely chopped mushrooms to be added later.*

Cut the meat in small pieces and fry, adding the chopped onions. When fried, add the wine and leave to reduce. Add the flour then the tomatoes moistened with a little stock. Add herbs and seasoning. Cook for forty-five minutes.

When cooked, take out all the pieces of meat and put through mincer, leaving a thick sauce. Add the mushrooms to the sauce.

[43]

FILLING

1 *finely chopped onion;* 1 *clove of garlic;* 4 *tablespoons of spinach puree;* 2 *chopped lambs brains;* 2 *egg yolks;* ½ *cup of grated parmesan cheese;* 3 *or* 4 *ozs of butter; stock for moistening.*

Fry the onion in a little butter, add the previously minced meat, the garlic, spinach puree, the brains and a little stock. Thicken with the egg yolks and some grated cheese.

Fill the pasta with this mixture. Lay the stuffed pasta on a buttered dish, sprinkled with cheese; pour in the sauce, sprinkle more cheese, add a few knobs of butter.

Cook in a medium oven for ten minutes.

SCOTCH KIPPERS

It gives me much pleasure to include the humble kipper among these special dishes. What is special about this dish is firstly the superiority of the best sort of kipper and secondly the trouble we take to cook this good fish properly.

This is the *only* way to cook a kipper.

You will need: real Scotch kippers, properly cured, not, horror of horrors, *painted*, a kettle full of boiling water and an enamel plate, one good dessertspoonful of butter.

Cut off the head and tail of the kippers. Place them on the enamel plate and rinse them in boiling water. Leave about a tablespoon full of hot water on the plate. Place a nob of butter on each kipper. Put them under a hot grill for about 4 or 5 minutes. Baste once or twice. When cooked glaze with the melted butter on the plate.

Perform the whole operation as fast as you can and enjoy the benefits of one of the few really special dishes that require the minimum of preparation.

EGG AND
VEGETABLE
DISHES

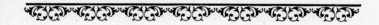
After so much rich food, it seems only fair to think about giving the stomach a rest.

Often, after cooking a fine banquet, I have enjoyed nothing so much as a light vegetable omelette. Just as it is good for you to enjoy your food, it is also bad to eat merely out of habit when you are tired or out of sorts. There must be many business-lunching husbands who would welcome a week-end of light but healthy food. There must be many wives too, I imagine, who do not welcome a heavy midday meal. The danger is that the wrong sort of snack can lead to debility, overweight and other disorders.

My motto on food, if feeling out of sorts is: *when in doubt, cut it out—but not altogether*. There are many valuable and delicious vegetable dishes which seem to be largely neglected in this country. Perhaps it is not thought quite proper to serve vegetables on their own.

On the subject of good health and sensible eating habits, I should like to quote Her Majesty the Queen.

For a member of the royal family, good health is indispensable. If you follow the Queen's progress in the newspapers you will find that she rarely has to cancel engagements for the minor but debilitating ailments that afflict most of us from time to time. Contrary to all the rumours I heard at the time, I have never known Her Majesty go on a specific diet.

Instead she eats from a varied diet which includes no fads or fancies, but all the essential nutriments.

All that has been said about Her Majesty's wonderful complexion and sparkling eyes is entirely true. She is, in fact one of the healthiest people I know. This is probably due to a splendid inherent constitution, plus plenty of fresh air and fresh foods. But there is one secret which may provide a clue to those glowing royal complexions—barley water.

All the royal family are addicted to barley water. The nursery consumed daily rations of it, it was always on the dining table. The Queen, usually drank it in preference to wine. In fact they all drank so much barley water that I felt there must be something in it and tried it myself.

When feeling at all out of sorts, a day or two on barley water is wonderfully purifying for the system, full of vitamins B and C, and sure enough, it does wonders for your skin.

This is one of the few recipes I took with me from Clarence House and in view of its beneficial effects, I hope I shall be forgiven.

BARLEY WATER

1 *teacup of pearl barley*   6 *oranges*
4 *pints of boiling water*   *demerera sugar to taste*
2 *lemons*

Put barley in a large saucepan, add the boiling water and simmer over a low heat with the lid on for one hour. Squeeze the fruit and keep the juice. Strain the water from the barley into a basin, adding the rind of one lemon and three oranges. Add sugar. Allow to stand until cold. Strain off the rinds and add the orange and lemon juice. Keep in refrigerator.

Every family has its own favourite recipes. These dishes are valuable indeed, whether they be Mum's apple pie or Auntie Flo's fishcakes, for they are more than just a meal they are part of the tradition of family life.

Buckingham Palace has its pancakes.

There isn't much tomato about them but they are always called

CRÊPES D'OEUFS AUX TOMATES

½ *lb flour*	1 *yolk*
1 *pint of milk*	*pinch of salt*
2 *whole eggs*	*nut oil for frying*

Filling: ½ *pint béchamel sauce; 3 hard-boiled eggs; cup of grated gruyere cheese; 1 tablespoon tomato sauce; pinch of sugar.*

Place in a basin, the flour, salt, two whole eggs and one yolk and mix well. Add the milk little by little, working the paste into the consistency of custard. Put enough nut oil in a small saucepan to coat the bottom and heat gently. When hot, pour the batter into the centre of the pan, one cup at a time. Work the mixture round to spread evenly and thinly over the pan. Adjust the heat to avoid burning. When set turn and cook the other side for one minute. Keep hot on a buttered baking sheet. Mix the béchamel sauce, chopped hard-boiled eggs, seasoning and sugar, and stuff the pancakes with the mixture. Spread the tomato sauce on top of the pancakes, sprinkle with cheese and brown under the grill.

MELON

Everyone has their favourite fruit. Mine is the Cheranties melon from Israel. Buy it on a beautiful day in June. It must be a Cheranties melon and it must come from Israel. Take no other.

Everything about the way you treat this melon must be perfect. So set a pretty table, if possible outdoors, and halve the melon with your best friend. Remove the pips with a silver spoon, chill and serve in your finest glass or china.

Eat and sit and think.

If your friend should feel that you have not worked hard enough you could fill the melon with mashed bananas and sieved strawberries. It will be delicious but not as good as the plain melon.

French beans are terribly expensive and sometimes cost about 22s. a pound. Asparagus is cheap and vulgar by comparison. Make sure your friends know this when you serve what you laughingly call:

BEANS AND BACON

1 *lb (or more) of French beans, topped and tailed;* ½ *lb streaky bacon.*

Boil the beans for ten minutes in a covered pan of salted water. Remove carefully with a spoon and tie in bundles like asparagus. Place them in a warm, buttered dish. While the beans are cooking be frying the bacon until golden brown, cut in strips and sprinkle on the beans.

CELERY IN CHEESE SAUCE

1 *root of celery per person*   *small cup of grated cheese*
½ *pint béchamel sauce to two*
    people

Clean and peel the celery. Cut in half and boil in salted water for half an hour. When boiled scoop out the centres and, adding some grated cheese to the béchamel sauce, pour over the celery, replacing the centres. Sprinkle with more grated cheese and put in a hot oven for five minutes.

Everyone has a recipe for stuffed pimentos. This is mine:

PIMENTOS WITH RISOTTO FILLING

1 *pimento per person*
½ *lb chickens' livers*
1 *cup of rice*
1 *large onion*
¼ *lb back bacon*
2 *ozs butter*
seasoning

Blanch the pimentos by bringing them to the boil in salted water. Slice off the tops and remove the seeds. Make the filling by mixing together the rice previously boiled in salted water, and the chopped bacon and onions fried gently together. Toss in the butter and fill the pimentos with the mixture. Cover with greaseproof paper and cook in a medium oven for ten minutes.

The following is a charming dish either as a first course or for a ladies' lunch.

ASPARAGUS TIPS IN MOUSSELINE SAUCE

1 *tin asparagus tips between*
   two
4 *tablespoons water*
3 *egg yolks*
¼ *lb cold butter*
dessertspoon salt

Whisk the egg yolks one by one into a pan of water and go on whisking until the whole thing is frothy. Bring to a heat just below boiling point. Whisk, lower the heat and whisk in the cold butter and salt.

Pour over the asparagus tips, and serve in a silver dish.

If someone you know is ill or miserable they might just prefer a bowl of very good soup. Not too ill or miserable to enjoy it though, as this soup is frankly quite a lot of trouble.

ASPARAGUS AND SPINACH SOUP

½ lb tin of asparagus tips
1 packet of frozen spinach
½ pint of good chicken or veal
  bone stock
½ tablespoon of cornflour mixed
  to a smooth cream with the
  asparagus juice
½ teaspoon of ground nutmeg

¼ pint of milk
¼ pint of cream
1 egg
1 tablespoon of grated parmesan or gruyere cheese
1 oz of butter
seasoning

Cut the spinach into slices and halve the asparagus tips.
Make a thick soup from the stock and cornflour mixed with
asparagus juice. Remove the soup from the heat when adding
the cornflour and whisk well. Let the soup simmer over a low
fire for ten minutes, add the spinach and let it simmer a further
five minutes. Season with pepper and salt, add the sugar and
nutmeg. In another saucepan, whisk the milk, cream and egg
together and add the soup to this mixture over a very low
heat. Still whisking, add the butter, the rest of the asparagus
juice, the tips and lastly the grated cheese.

Do not boil, but serve the soup nice and hot.

This should do your friend a lot of good.

Together with barley water, there is really nothing more
soothing for the stomach after a digestive upset than:

OATMEAL PORRIDGE

1 cup of pinhead oatmeal
1 pint of water

pinch of salt
teaspoon demerera sugar

Soak the oatmeal in water and bring to the boil. Add salt
and sugar and continue boiling for an hour.

Serve with salt or sugar according to your side of the Border.

Once or twice a year on a very hot day when there is someone special coming for tea try this:

CHINA TEA WITH ORANGE

2 *teaspoons of china tea to one*
  pint of water
3 *oranges*
ice cubes

the juice of a lemon
3 *tablespoons of demerera*
  sugar

Make the tea with boiling water and stand to draw. Slice one orange thinly and squeeze the juice from the other two. Add lemon juice and sugar. Strain the juice into the tea. Pour out and serve with floated slices of orange and some ice cubes.

In the interests of health people are keen nowadays on pure foods and cooking aids and will go to some trouble to find them.

One uses the following three basic ingredients so much in cooking that I think it is worthwhile tracking down the purest kind in both flavour and composition:

Salt—I use Maldon Crystal Salt which is almost perfectly pure chloride of sodium free from other chemicals. Or Tidman's Sea Salt which is the pure evaporation of sea water.

Pepper—best results are found by using whole peppercorns, white or black in a pepper mill. For unadulterated ground pepper I use a brand called Mignonette. Cayenne pepper is a very useful flavouring agent but is quite different from ordinary pepper as it is made from ground chillies.

Oil—many people regard olive oil as the best in edible oils, but I choose groundnut oil even for mayonnaise in preference to olive oil which is inclined to have a distinctive after-taste. Sunflower oil has a slightly strong flavour, but has a lower fat value than other oils and is recommended for cooking purposes in preference to animal fats by people suffering from heart conditions.

CAKES AND
PUDDINGS

CAKES AND PUDDINGS

Despite, or probably because of, increased urbanisation and the mass production of food, I have a strong feeling that the domestic arts are flourishing again.

I know a high-powered career woman in the heart of London who spends one evening a week baking her own bread. A glamorous model surprisingly produces a delicious home-baked sponge on a Sunday afternoon. The country-woman scorns the instant cake mixtures and turns out a fragrant fruit cake made from a recipe that has been handed down from her grandmother.

There is a certain satisfaction contained in the smell of baking, the look of a well risen cake, that nothing else can quite approach. It is a woman's way of saying that she cares for her family and no shop-bought cake can say it for her.

Perhaps my happiest memories of Clarence House are of teatime in the nursery, in those carefree but numbered days when the Queen was Princess Elizabeth. She would spend the afternoon playing on the lawn with her two small children; carefully folding up the rug and taking in the toys when it was time for tea. Tea was always in the sun-filled nursery, informal and gay with Prince Charles chatting excitedly about the day's events. Even illustrious visitors like foreign Kings and Queens failed to make it anything but family tea with everyone sharing in the banana sandwiches and sponge cake.

Teatime with the Queen Mother and Princess Margaret was quite different, they took it at a small table laid with a white cloth in the drawing room. Then they laid another tablecloth on the floor on which the dogs were given their meal.

My most popular cake with the royal family was a rich chocolate cake made to my own recipe. Everyone seemed to like this cake and it went everywhere. By special request I have sent it off to Windsor, Balmoral and Sandringham and the Queen Mother asked for it for her birthday. Here it is:

CHOCOLATE CAKE MADE WITH ORANGE MARMALADE

8 *ozs butter*
8 *ozs caster sugar*
1 *tablespoon orange marmalade*
8 *ozs plain flour*

2 *teaspoons baking powder*
2 *ozs ground sweet almonds*
5 *eggs (separated)*
6 *ozs chocolate Menier*

Beat butter and sugar to light cream. Add egg yolks and marmalade. Stir in chocolate which has been melted over a low heat. Add flour, baking powder and almonds. Whip egg whites stiff and mix in lightly. Pour into greased 2 lb cake tin and bake in a slow oven for one hour and fifteen minutes.

When cool, cut in half, fill and ice top with the following mixture:

4 *ozs butter ;* 8 *ozs icing sugar ;* 2 *tablespoons coffee essence (instant coffee mixed with 2 tablespoons of warm water will do).*

Cream all the ingredients together and warm slightly for spreading.

The cake looks nice decorated with pistachio nuts.

Here are some light buns suitable for nursery tea. I call them Chilean buns because I had the recipe from the Chilean

Embassy after a member of the royal family had enjoyed them there for tea.

CHILEAN BUNS

1 *teacup plain flour*	½ *teaspoon salt*
1 *tablespoon butter*	½ *cup of milk*
1 *teaspoon baking powder*	

Mix all the ingredients together into a hard dough and roll into a long sausage. Cut into small bun shapes, place on a greased baking sheet and cross them with the back of a knife. Place in a hot oven for five to ten minutes.

Everybody's main fear with a soufflé is that it may not soufflé, which is why, perhaps, there has been a decline in this delicious dish. The following is a never-fail soufflé. It is not a fussy soufflé and you can even open the oven and inspect progress if anxious, with no fatal results.

PRUNE SOUFFLÉ

½ *lb dried prunes*	5 *whites of eggs*
¼ *lb dried apricots (if using tinned fruit, double the amounts)*	4 *tablespoons caster sugar*
	½ *teaspoon vanilla essence*
	1 *pint water*

Soak the fruit overnight. Put the fruit into a pan of water, bring to the boil and simmer until soft. Strain the juice into a basin and remove the stones from the prunes. Remove skin from the fruit. Grease soufflé dish with butter. Whip up egg whites into a stiff froth and fold in two tablespoons sugar very gently. Then mix together the fruit and juice, two tablespoons caster sugar and vanilla essence. Gently fold the egg whites into the mixture, pour into the soufflé dish and bake in a slow oven for half an hour.

Serve with single cream or vanilla ice cream that has been dished up fifteen minutes beforehand so that it has become slightly softened.

Cooking for royalty is an honour, but it is no use pretending that the work in a royal household is not demanding. It would be easy if all one had to do was produce an inspired menu for royalty and bask in the glory of it all. But real life in royal households is not like that. In my time at Clarence House there were between eighty and a hundred *un*royal mouths to feed as well. Most lunch times there were about three different menus going at the same time.

First the nursery, whose menus were simple but needed careful preparation. Then the royal lunch, usually with guests. Next the staff who ate substantially from a different menu. There were also the ever-hungry policemen who ate after the staff and enjoyed whatever was going.

Like any harassed housewife, I relied on some dishes which were quick and easy to make, but good of their kind. One of the most useful was:

PRINCE CHARLES' SUMMER PUDDING

1 *pint fruit juice according to*   3 *tablespoons of cornflour*
season   *mixed with water*
sugar to taste

Make the fruit juice with 1 lb fresh fruit in 1 pint of water, add sugar, bring to the boil and simmer for five minutes. Boil fruit juice with cornflour for three minutes and pour into glasses. Serve with single cream.

Another nursery pudding which is also easy to do but sophisticated enough for the dining-room on a warm summer's evening is this:

ICE CREAM WITH BLACKCURRANT SAUCE

1 *block of vanilla ice cream*   2 *tablespoons cornflour*
1 *pint blackcurrant juice*   *sugar*

Heat the blackcurrant juice, add sugar to taste, thicken with two tablespoons cornflour and boil for two to three minutes. Cool off and pour over the ice cream to serve.

Here is an apple meringue sponge with a difference. The difference I think, lies mainly in the lightness of the sponge and the cream filling which flavours the cake if left to soak overnight.

APPLE MERINGUE SPONGE

4 *eggs*   2 *teaspoons baking powder*
equal quantity in weight of   2 *ozs cornflour*
  sugar
half the weight of the eggs in
  plain flour

Filling: ¼ *pint single cream;* ½ *teaspoon vanilla essence;* 4 *cooking apples; sugar to taste.*

Meringue: 3 *whites of eggs;* 3 *tablespoons of caster sugar; grated rind of half a lemon.*

For the sponge, whip the whole eggs and sugar together for twenty-five minutes with a whisk or ten minutes with electric beaters. Mix the flour and baking powder together and sieve, mix with sugar and eggs. Put onto two flat, greased tins and bake in a hot oven for twenty minutes. Remove and turn out and when cold place in a flat fireproof dish. Mix cream with vanilla essence and spread over the cake.

Peel, core and cook the apples with sugar and make into a not too wet puree. Spread the puree on top of the cake.

Whip up the whites of eggs and fold in the sugar after beating, also the lemon rind. Pile it up on top of the apple and bake in a low oven for half an hour.

Keep overnight.

Home baked bread is both impressive and delicious and not nearly so difficult to make as the amateur might suppose. And once you have made your own bread it is hard to return to the mostly mediocre shop bought variety.

Try these two recipes one wet afternoon; and tea-time, with the smell of these sweetly scented loaves, will brighten the day.

SWEET LOAF

1½ *lb brown flour*	*teaspoon carraway seeds*
½ *lb white flour*	*teaspoon of salt*
1 *pint of milk (can be sour)*	2 *oz of lard*
½ *teacup of golden syrup*	*white flour for sprinkling*
2 *oz yeast*	*teacup of water mixed with*
tablespoon chopped orange peel	*teaspoon golden syrup*

Warm milk to blood heat and add the brown flour. Stir well and work in the lard. Beat into a dough and add the yeast diluted in water, also the syrup, salt, orange peel and carraway seeds. Stir into a stodgy dough with electric beaters until the mixture is shiny and no longer sticking to the bowl. Sprinkle some flour over the mixture and let it rise in a warm place. Knead again if the dough is not stodgy enough and add a little more flour. Roll out on a floured table. Fill 1 lb tins to the halfway mark and let it rise almost to the top. Brush over with the syrupy water and prick three times with skewer.

Bake in a moderate oven and brush over again with the syrup water after half an hour. Bake for a further hour.

RYE TIN LOAF

1 lb of rye flour
½ pint of yoghurt or sour milk
½ lb of white flour
1 teaspoon of bicarbonate of soda
½ teaspoon of baking powder
1 teaspoon of salt
2 tablespoons of melted margarine

Mix all together to a firm dough. Grease an oblong tin and place the mixture in a very slow oven for twenty minutes. Increase the heat and bake for another forty minutes.

This loaf can develop into a craze. Last time I baked it, I was asked for it again and again until a royal tour or holiday or something intervened. This was fortunate, as on the last occasion I baked it at Birkhall, eighty people including all the Ladies in Waiting arrived for tea.

There is nothing nicer than pancakes, if you have a hungry family to feed. I often used to make these pancakes after the royal family had been out shooting for the day at Balmoral.

SWEET PANCAKES

3 eggs
4 ozs flour
½ tablespoon sugar
pinch of salt
1 cup of milk
½ cup of cold water
½ cup of cream

Beat the eggs with the water. Sift the flour, sugar and salt and add to the beaten egg. Mix well to a smooth paste. Then add the milk and cream. Allow the mixture to stand for half an hour.

Cook the pancakes in butter until golden brown. The pancakes are very good filled with vanilla ice cream or soufflé mixture. Or with crushed strawberries or raspberries.

I have a low opinion of most mass-produced ice cream. At any rate it has little to do with real cream. The following recipe will make you realize what you have been missing.

BOMBE GLACÉE

4 yolks of eggs
2 tablespoons sugar
vanilla essence to taste

½ pint double cream
½ pint milk

Put the egg yolks in a saucepan together with the sugar. Boil the milk separately and add it to the egg mixture, gradually whisking all the time. Keep over a low heat but do not let the mixture boil. Whisk until it thickens like a custard. Remove from heat and whisk until cold. Whisk cream and add to the mixture, pour into an ice tray or mould and put into the freezing compartment of the refrigerator until set.

PRUNE PUDDING

1 lb tinned or soaked prunes
1 oz ground almonds
1 lemon
¼ lb butter
2 tablespoons plain flour

½ pint cream
½ lb caster sugar
6 eggs
vanilla essence to taste

Mix egg yolks and sugar together for fifteen minutes. Add cream, flour and butter and whisk over heat until the mixture thickens. Move saucepan from heat and continue whisking until the mixture cools. Add juice of lemon and grated rind and vanilla essence. Then add the beaten egg whites. Lay the prunes (stoned) and a little grated lemon rind on the bottom of a greased fireproof dish, pour mixture on top and bake in a moderate oven for one hour. Turn the pudding out on to a dish so that the prunes are uppermost. Serve with whipped cream and sprinkle the top with chopped almonds.

Can be eaten hot or cold.

If you like dark, stodgy Christmas cake, the next recipe is not for you. This is the cake that the royal family enjoyed. I would bake this cake on 13th of November when all the royal puddings were prepared, keep it and send it off to Sandringham for Christmas day. This cake is lighter in appearance and texture than the traditional kind but will keep equally well for a year or more.

McKEE'S CHRISTMAS CAKE

1 lb of butter
1½ lbs of plain flour
1 lb of caster sugar
1 lb of currants
1 lb of sultanas
½ lb of stoned raisins
2 tablespoons of orange marmalade

¼ lb of candied peel
10 eggs
pinch of salt
1 tablespoon of black treacle
½ teaspoon of nutmeg
2 tablespoons of rum
1 teaspoon of vanilla essence
½ teaspoon of almond essence

Stir butter and sugar together until creamy. Add marmalade and treacle. Drop in the egg yolks one at a time and a tablespoon of flour to each yolk, stirring all the time. Mix all the fruit in with the flour. Add nutmeg and pinch of salt. Add to the mixture with the essences and, last of all, the rum. Beat the egg whites to a stiff snow and fold in. Line a tin with paper, grease it well, fill it with the mixture and bake in a slow oven for two to three hours.

FISH DISHES

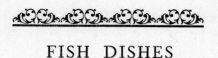

FISH DISHES

If I had to exist on one particular food in preference to all others, I know I would choose fish. Fish is nutritious, inexpensive and versatile, yet the majority of families eat it only once a week.

The royal family have fish every day, mostly in the evening when a fish course is always included in the dinner. The fish for the royal residences is delivered fresh from Billingsgate every morning as, together with staff, and members of the household, we constituted a wholesale order. Milk, cream and vegetables came from the farm at Windsor, game from Balmoral, and meat from a small butcher in Staines. Groceries came from that well-known store in Piccadilly and I also made regular trips into Soho for the sort of things you can only find in that district. I had a free hand with the housekeeping though I had to make out the accounts in a double entry ledger every week.

In the days when I was at Clarence House, strict rationing was still in force and although we were supplemented by game and poultry from the royal estates we had problems just like everyone else. For instance, the staff did not much like game, then there were the royal guests, several times a week, who did not unfortunately, bring their ration books with them.

I had great recourse to fish and luckily, the royal family were fond of it.

The following is a distinctly inaustere dish, suitable for about six people on some rather special occasion.

FILLET OF DOVER SOLE REGINA

2 *Dover sole, weighing about 1¾ lb each*
2 *cooked lobster, about 1½ lb each*
½ *bottle of champagne or dry white wine*
1 *lb of lemon sole fillets*
3 *eggs*
6 *ozs of butter*
½ *pint of single cream*
¼ *pint of milk*
seasoning and a pinch of sugar
1 *oz of flour*
(serves six)

Skin and fillet the Dover soles. Cover some of the bones and heads with half the wine and some water, bring to the boil and simmer for half an hour. Make a force-meat from the lemon sole and 3 ozs of butter by passing through the mincer three times. In another bowl mix the cream, milk and three yolks of eggs and stir into the force-meat. Dissect the lobsters and add any small bits and pieces of lobster to the fish cream.

Rinse and dry the filleted Dover sole and season well. Keeping the underside on the inside, roll and stuff the fillets with the force-meat. Place in a buttered fireproof dish with the rest of the wine and cover with greaseproof paper. Poach in a hot oven for twenty minutes.

Remove the fillets and drain. Reduce the liquid by simmering. Make a sauce with the flour, 1 oz of butter, and about a pint of fish stock, cook until it thickens. Reduce heat and while simmering add the reduced liquid from the fillets. Remove from heat and strain the sauce and stir in 2 ozs of cold butter. Place the cut lobster on top of each fillet and coat with the sauce. Garnish round the dish with the meat from the lobster claws and some parsley.

Serve with button mushrooms steamed in butter, and new potatoes.

The following is a dish of the utmost simplicity, but one which repays careful attention to detail. The boning of the fish is easily done if a nice, clean slit is made in the stomach, and the backbone removed from the tail end.

TRUITE EN BLEU ROYALE

6 *blue trout weighing 6 ozs*	1 *oz flour*
each	*salt and pepper*
½ *lb butter*	*Tarragon sauce (page* 18)

The flesh of the blue trout should be a firm whitish pink. Remove scales, fins and the backbone but not the head. Remove as many small bones as possible. Rinse well and drain on a towel for ten minutes. Open and season then close. Melt butter in frying pan. Dip the trout in white flour and cook gently in the butter until golden brown, about five minutes each side. When cooked place in a dish with a little butter and cover with greaseproof paper before serving.

Serve with Tarragon sauce, cucumber salad, dressed with Tarragon vinegar and piped creamed potatoes.

One of the pleasantest interludes during my time with British royalty was a stay at Balmoral while the Queen Mother was there with Prince Charles and Princess Anne. This was virtually in the nature of a holiday for me as the Buckingham Palace staff were there, and such is the below stairs protocol that I would not have dared bake so much as a cake without a formal request from the chef.

Towards the end of July there is a great upheaval in royal households. Preparations for the annual holiday at Balmoral starts a week or so beforehand. Pots, pans, china and utensils, everything in fact except the Buckingham Palace stove is packed up and sent ahead. On the appointed day the staffs of Buckingham Palace and Clarence House meet on the station at Kings Cross and wait for a special train that takes them to Ballater.

On my first journey I remember being amazed that even Buckingham Palace could hold so many people until I realized that many were taking their wives, families and domestic animals as well. The scene reminded me of some King from ancient history moving camp.

Whenever the Queen goes to Balmoral, Windsor or Sandringham, the chief chef Mr. Aubrey, his four principal assistants and a staff that varies from two hundred to fifty, according to the length of the stay, go with her. The remaining staff at Buckingham Palace then go on a system known as board wages. Board wages is an old-fashioned system whereby the staff can either eat in the Palace or take the money to buy their own food. At the Palace there are six male chefs and a staff of about five hundred, all of whom have to be fed. It would be impossible to keep all the royal palaces fully staffed, so every now and again there is this great move.

At Balmoral all the royal family lead an outdoor life, but of the ladies, it is the Queen Mother who is the most energetic. Her great passion is for salmon fishing, and this she does with great concentration for hours on end. There is certainly nothing dilettante about the Queen Mother's fishing. She puts on waders and old clothes and is out to catch the biggest salmon she can find. She likes no interruption and takes with her only the simplest of cold picnics.

Once, after two whole days of concentrated fishing, the Queen Mother presented me with two salmon one of which must have weighed about 20 lbs. 'Do what you like with them' she said. 'Why not give the staff a treat?'

As there was only one rather small, and very old-fashioned refrigerator at Balmoral, I sent the large salmon up to Clarence House to be put in the deep freeze to await a staff treat on my return, and cooked the smaller one according to the following recipe.

BALMORAL SALMON

1 *salmon*	3 *or* 4 *slices of onion*
1 *carrot*	*parsley*
1 *dessertspoon vinegar*	2 *teaspoons salt*
10 *white peppercorns*	

Rinse salmon and drain and place in a large saucepan with the sliced carrot, onion, peppercorns, salt and vinegar. Cover with water and bring to the boil. Reduce heat and keep hot for five minutes. When dishing up remove skin and bone without breaking the flesh and drain well. Cover with sauce Citron (p. 24), garnish with parsley and serve with small boiled potatoes and cucumber salad.

The following recipes for crevettes can be used either as a fish course in a dinner party menu or as the main course of a light luncheon. In both recipes it is the pinch of cayenne pepper that gives the extra kick to these delicious little fishes.

PRAWNS PIQUANT

½ pint of Dublin Bay prawns to each person
½ pint of white sauce
½ glass of sherry or white wine
1 tablespoon of tomato sauce or teaspoon of extract
1 tablespoon of Heinz mayonnaise
½ teaspoon of salt
pinch of cayenne pepper and pinch of sugar

To the white sauce add the sherry, tomato sauce, mayonnaise, salt, cayenne pepper and sugar, blend well and simmer for two to three minutes. Pour over the prawns and garnish with parsley.

CASSOULET DE CREVETTES

shrimps (½ pint per person)
2 tablespoons dry white wine
½ pint of fish stock
2 tablespoons of cream
1½ ozs of butter
1 oz flour
pinch of cayenne pepper, teaspoon of salt

Make the sauce by melting butter then adding flour until absorbed. Pour in fish stock and seasoning and mix over a low heat. Add cream, and stir until the mixture thickens. Stir in the wine and pour the sauce over the shrimps.

Serve in a pretty dish with melba toast.

Here is a fish course, very simple ingredients, an easy method, but try it on your friends and like as not they will ask for the recipe. This is how we treat our fish in Sweden.

CUTLETS OF PLAICE IN BUTTER
for 2 persons

4 fillets of plaice
½ a lemon
¼ lb of butter
2 beaten eggs
flour, salt, pepper

Skin, rinse and dry the fillets. Season with salt and pepper. Spread some flour on greaseproof paper. Place half the butter in a frying pan and place over a low heat. Heat gradually but do not let the butter turn brown. Fold the fillets in half so that the inside is on the outside, turn them in the flour and dip in the beaten egg. Drop them in the hot butter and fry about three minutes on each side until golden brown.

Dish up and garnish with lemon slices, fried parsley and peas, or spinach natural.

Turbot is a good rich fish and, served according to the following recipe as a main course, would only need a clear soup beforehand and perhaps a savoury afterwards to make a fine dinner party.

TURBOT WITH HORSERADISH SAUCE

2 *lbs of middle cut of turbot to*   1 *tablespoon of flour*
  four people   1½ *ozs of cold butter*
1 *pint of boiling water*   1 *dessertspoon of salt*
8 *pimento peppercorns*   ½ *a grated horseradish*

Cut the turbot into cutlets about 2 inches thick without removing the bone. Place the cutlets into boiling water, add seasoning. Cover with greaseproof paper and steam for ten to fifteen minutes. Strain the fish stock and thicken with the flour for a thick sauce, add more seasoning, to taste and simmer for five minutes. Remove from heat and whisk the cold butter in little by little. Keep hot. Carefully remove skin and bones from the fish and place the cutlets on a dish. Cover the fish with some of the sauce. Serve the rest separately with the grated horseradish stirred in.

Serve with plain boiled potatoes in a white napkin.

I hope I am not alone in my admiration for the haddock. Haddock is a clean nutritious fish with an individual nutty flavour, but I have a feeling it is regarded as the poor relation of the fish family.

The following recipes, once you have tried them, may do something to restore the status of this good-living fish.

I have served the following recipe throughout my cooking career and out of all my fish dishes this is the one I cook most frequently in my own home.

GRILLED HADDOCK SPECIAL
for 2 persons

2 fillets of haddock
1 oz of butter
¼ pint of creamy milk

4 tomatoes
½ lb of creamed potatoes
salt, pepper and flour

Rinse and dry the haddock thoroughly. Cut the haddock into four pieces. Season with pepper and salt. Melt the butter and dip the fillets in the butter on both sides and then in the flour and again in the butter. Place them in a buttered dish ready for grilling. Baste once or twice under the grill. When coloured, pour the milk over the fish, remove from grill and place the dish containing the fish over a low heat on top of the stove to simmer for two to three minutes. Reduce the milky sauce a little so that the haddock is glazed. Skin and halve the tomatoes and remove the pips. Place them on a fireproof dish with a small knob of butter, season and pipe the creamed potatoes into the tomatoes.

The following recipe proves that haddock can behave itself in the grand manner at a smart dinner party.

CRÈME DE HADDOCK FUMÉ TARTARE
serves four to six people

1½ lbs of smoked haddock
½ lb of white bread softened in
milk
¼ lb butter
4 eggs

¼ pint of good milk
1 level dessertspoon of salt
pinch of sugar
½ teaspoon of pepper

Remove the skin and bones of the haddock and put it through a mincer with the butter three times. Add the bread panade previously made with hot milk and fresh bread and allowed to cool. Mix well with the creamed fish. Whisk in the egg yolks, milk, pepper, salt and sugar. Add all these ingredients a little at a time, stirring hard for about half an hour when the ingredients will resemble a smooth cream. Then add the four egg whites which should have been beaten to a very stiff froth and blend in well with the creamed fish. Fill a buttered basin or mould with the mixture and cover with greaseproof paper or foil. Steam for one hour on a low heat in boiling water taking care not to let the water penetrate the fish cream, keeping the saucepan or bain marie firmly covered.

When cooked, turn out on a dish and serve with a border of boiled rice, garnished with shrimps or prawns.

Serve tartare sauce separately (recipe see page 20).

PICNICS AND SMÖRGÅSBORD

PICNICS AND SMÖRGÅSBORD

There are two enormous advantages to eating out of doors: one physical, the other psychological. Firstly, eating in the open air relaxes the pressures under which most of us live and keens the appetite.

Secondly, unwrapping the food from a well-appointed picnic hamper enhances the flavour and stimulates the imagination. Food, like women, benefits from a little mystery, which is why the contents of a picnic hamper should always be kept secret.

I have many ideas about picnics and none of them include sandwiches. It is true that sandwiches travel well, but so do hundreds of other foods that can be eaten out of doors. In fact, nowadays with the splendid selection of plastic containers there are few things that cannot travel.

The picnic food at Balmoral is transported in big, old-fashioned hampers, packed into the back of a shooting brake or Land Rover. Those capacious, laundry basket type of hampers take a lot of beating. With good packing and a polythene top, even a fruit fool can arrive intact.

Careful preparation is the secret of a good picnic. What people want when they sit down in the great outdoors is *instant* food. Poultry and meat should be jointed or carved beforehand, for instance, so that the food can be unpacked and eaten right away.

[81]

I was accustomed to doing this anyway for the royal family, as they do not carve and all food is sent into the dining room ready for serving.

Here are just a few ideas which can be enlarged upon. On the subject of good picnics I will say at once that I owe a lot to aspic jelly.

ASPIC LIVER PATÉ

2 *lbs of calves liver*
1 *lb of fatty bacon*
6 *eggs*
½ *pint of single cream*
2 *tablespoons of flour*
3 *or 4 sieved anchovies*
1 *tablespoon of tomato sauce*

1 *tablespoon of brandy*
pepper, salt and a pinch of sugar
1 *pint aspic jelly*
1 *tablespoon of sherry or white wine*

Mince liver and three quarters of the bacon together and put it through a sieve or in a mixer. Mix the eggs, cream, flour and seasoning in a basin and add little by little to the liver mixture, stirring all the time. Add the sieved anchovies, the tomato sauce and the brandy. Bake, in an oblong bread tin lined and covered with bacon and wrapped in foil, in a medium oven for two hours. Allow the paté to cool then remove from tin and wash the tin. Add the wine to the aspic. Replace the paté, cover with aspic jelly and allow to cool.

The following is more of a happy memory than a recipe, which is how good food should be thought of when it is related to a beautiful day, a perfect setting and happy people. It was consumed outside a disused Victorian Palace belonging to the royal family near Loch N'Gair and it was the sort of day on which you count your blessings.

[82]

ROYAL PLATTER

a fillet of beef
a little gelatine
fresh lettuce

small braised onions
tomatoes
horseradish sauce

Roast the fillet of beef, fifteen minutes to the pound in a hot oven, decreasing the heat slightly after the first half-hour. Add a little gelatine stock to the natural juices when cooked and as it cools, spoon the juice over the beef so that it is glazed in jelly.

The beef was then sliced and rested on fresh lettuce leaves. With it I served small braised onions, slightly glazed, and skinned and pipped tomatoes, filled with horseradish sauce mixed with cream.

This was accompanied by a *mixed vegetable salad* made from:

½ *a shredded white cabbage; 2 grated carrots; ½ a cucumber cut in strips; 1 chopped dessert apple; small pieces of leek cut in thin rings; 1 tin of petit pois; 1 tablespoon of chopped capers; 2 or 3 ounces of pickled cucumber and gherkins cut in rings.*

The salad dressing is my own version which I always keep by me winter and summer. It needs shaking up in a bottle before serving.

McKEE'S SALAD DRESSING

½ *cup of Tarragon vinegar*
1 *tablespoon of nut oil*
½ *teaspoon of dry mustard dissolved in some vinegar*

½ *teaspoon of pepper*
½ *teaspoon salt*
pinch of sugar

Stir the ingredients together then whisk a little.

Another cold joint, highly convenient for picnics is:

BEST END OF NECK

1 *best end of neck of English*
  lamb containing six cutlets
1 *clove of garlic*

1 *pint of aspic jelly*
tomatoes and mint jelly

Insert the garlic into the joint and roast in a hot oven for a half-hour in its own fat. Remove from pan and remove garlic. Chine and separate the cutlets with a sharp knife. Put together again and coat with aspic when cool. Serve with halved tomatoes filled with mint jelly.

With this I serve one of my favourite accompaniments:

CUCUMBER SALAD

You can either peel the cucumbers or not, according to taste. Cut the cucumber into thin slices and put in a basin. Season with pepper and salt, a teaspoon of sugar and some chopped mint. Let it soak in a tablespoon (or more according to the amount of cucumber) of Tarragon vinegar

On this same theme of meat cooled in its own juices with a reinforced jelly and served with an interesting salad, there are many other variations.

Veal, for instance cooled in a lightly spiced jelly and served with:

CAULIFLOWER SALAD

1 *large cauliflower*
1 *lemon*
nut oil
tarragon vinegar

seasoning
dry mustard
chopped chives or parlsey

Cut the cauliflower into bouquets and boil in water with the juice of the lemon. Remove before the cauliflower becomes soft, drain in a napkin and while still hot put in a basin. Mix some McKee's salad dressing, pour onto the cauliflower and let it soak. Garnish with chives or parsley.

With cold gammon,

FRUIT SALAD

Squeeze the juice of one grapefruit and an orange. Slice some bananas, apples, grapes, orange and grapefruit and leave to soak overnight in the juice. Add some sugar to taste.

Take this dish on a picnic and watch it vanish:—

CHICKEN CREAM IN ASPIC

4 *lb of boiling chicken*
½ *lb of bacon*
4 *tablespoons of breadcrumbs*
1 *pint cream*
a little warm milk
½ *pint of aspic jelly mixed with a tablespoon of medium*

sweet white wine
1 *teaspoon sugar*
seasoning
cucumber, olives, for decoration

Cut away meat from chicken. Put three times through the mincer. Soften the breadcrumbs with warm milk and mix together. Add pepper, salt, sugar and gradually add the cream, stirring all the time. Line the tin with bacon. Spread in the mixture and cover with rashers. Steam in water, either in the oven or on top of the stove, taking care that it does not boil over. Cook for an hour. Turn out when cool, clean the tin, decorate the bottom with cut olives and cucumber, replace the chicken cream and pour over the aspic jelly. Cool and turn out onto a bed of lettuce.

Can be made with veal instead of chicken.

A nice complement to this dish is the following sauce with lettuce and hardboiled eggs.

SALAD SAUCE WITH EGGS

½ *teaspoon of dry mustard*   4 *hardboiled eggs*
½ *cup of vinegar*   ½ *cup of cream*
pepper, salt and pinch of sugar   *lettuce and chives*

Mix the mustard with the vinegar, pepper, salt and sugar
to a smooth paste. Sieve the hardboiled egg yolks into a small
basin, blend in some cream and stir well. Add the vinaigrette
sauce gradually, stirring all the time, and finish with the rest
of the cream.

Pour over a salad of lettuce and chopped chives and
sprinkle with the chopped whites of eggs.

The nice thing about Scandinavian Smörgasbord is that
they are so versatile. For a buffet supper you can make them
large and juicy, using fairly substantial ingredients such as
small frikadellars, minced beefsteaks, saute'd kidneys, mushrooms, slices of beef and so on. As cocktail canapé's, make
them smaller on interesting bread and concentrate on making
a contrast both of flavour and appearance on each smorgasbord. That is to say, on a piece of brown bread I might sieve
the yolk of a hardboiled egg, placing it in the middle of the
bread, surround the yellow yolk with chopped white of egg
and garnish with an anchovy. This is rather a simple example
but it illustrates the contrast.

There are no exact rules or recipes for making up Smörgåsbord. It is a matter of inspiration and piquant ingredients,
bearing in mind the central theme of contrast.

First, some ingredients. If I were preparing at able of
Smörgåsbord I should start with the following ingredients:

Thinly sliced ham; cooked salmon; crabmeat; smoked eel;
herrings in marinade; liver paté (recipe page 82); shrimps;

sardines; anchovies; mussels; hard-boiled eggs; asparagus in
vinaigrette sauce; small new beetroots in sweetened tarragon
vinegar; fruit salad; cucumber salad; celery; radishes; spring
onions; tinned red and yellow pimentos; watercress; lettuce,
parsley and chopped chives for decoration and plenty of home
made mayonnaise (recipe page 19).

For a professional look the mayonnaise can be piped.
Cut brown, white and rye bread into circles, squares or
triangles. It should not be too thin if it is to support some of
the moisture or more substantial garnishes, but not doorsteps
of course.

To start you off:

Fold ham slices into cornets and fill either with a little fruit
salad and mayonnaise or with mayonnaise and asparagus
tips, place on a lettuce leaf on white buttered bread.

Mix some crab meat, chopped hardboiled eggs and
mayonnaise together. Place on dark brown bread and
decorate with piped mayonnaise and chopped chives. The
same can be done with a salmon mixture spread on bread
and decorated with cucumber slices.

The appearance of the Smörgåsbord table is important
too. One thing we always have in Sweden is a large cucumber
with the middle scooped out like a canoe and filled with
Russian salad. Celery sticks filled with Danish Blue cheese
also look decorative and are delicious to eat.

At hot Smörgåsbord parties, the guests walk around with
little plates and forks helping themselves, and the hostess
works hard.

I have only to think of a Smörgåsbord party to wish I was
actually giving one. Now at this minute I would offer: *calves*
kidneys sautéd in port wine. Anchovies rolled in breadcrumbs

and deep fried. Little omelettes stuffed with white sauce and asparagus tips or creamed sweetbreads. Small onions filled with chopped-up meat, braised in brown butter sauce and glazed in a little sugared aspic.

Another occasion might produce a completely different Smorgasbord table. In fact, no two parties are ever alike.

One thing that never alters, however, is the traditional hot cup always offered at Christmas parties in Sweden, Jule Grogg. I cannot think of it without seeing the big red Christmas candles, and drawn curtains in a gaily decorated room.

Many people in Britain regard wine cups and the like with distrust. They prefer their drinks straight. They have good reason. Most of us have suffered at one time or another from the indiscriminate cup where everything is mixed together with dire results. The other familiar offering is a sickly lemonade type substitute that gets nobody anywhere!

The following prescription for Swedish Grogg is especially suitable for consumption on the premises of draughty English country houses on a cold winter's day. In Sweden we always drink it on Christmas morning. In England I can imagine it going down particularly well as a stirrup cup on Boxing Day, or at almost any time during a freeze-up. For a Swedish style party, serve it with Smörgåsbord.

JULE GROGG

½ *bottle of Vodka*
½ *bottle of Port Wine*
10 *cardamom seeds*
1 *oz of muscatel raisins*
1 *small cinnamon stick*

4 *cloves*
1 *oz of blanched and skinned sweet almonds*
2 *lumps of sugar or one table-spoon of demerera sugar*

Pour the wine and Vodka into a silver or stainless steel saucepan and warm until hot. Rinse the raisins in hot water and add to the Grogg together with the almonds, cardamom seeds, cloves and cinnamon stick. Cover and heat then add the sugar. Just before the drink is ready to serve, set fire to it with a match, burn quickly and extinguish with the lid.

Serve and drink as hot as possible . . . Skol.

LUNCH AND
DINNER MENUS

It can't be wrong to want to please people with your cooking. And one asks for nothing in return except that people should enjoy themselves. The general mood of health, happiness and benevolence bestowed by a good meal is ample thanks to the cook.

I once worked in a castle in Sweden where they toasted the cook in champagne between every course. A charming idea, but frankly the cooking suffered in the end.

Nowadays most intelligent women are wonderful cooks. But many from time to time feel the need to provide something rather impressive for a special occasion. Perhaps they have to entertain their husband's business friends, or in-laws, or some rather grand acquaintances or maybe just someone they love.

Sometimes it is necessary to pull out all the stops and do better than your best. How do you define the thin line between good cooking and making a good impression?

I don't like showy cooking myself; but I can't pretend that I haven't always been influenced by the circumstances of a special occasion.

People often ask me if I was made nervous by the illustrious names on the guest list when I was cooking at Clarence House.

Well I would have been of course, if I had known who was

to be there beforehand. But often the Comptroller's guest list, issued a fortnight in advance, simply stated the number of guests to a particular meal. I was fortified by that, and told myself they were just people. Once there were four Queens to lunch. Luckily I didn't know until afterwards when I received a message that the royal ladies had thoroughly enjoyed my sole veronique. Had I known I might have been influenced to try something grander. Yet sole veronique at its best, is certainly a dish to set before a Queen.

Another time when the Queen Mother and Princess Margaret gave a joint party attended by the Queen and Prince Philip the guest list went like this: The Duchess of Kent, Mr. Billy Wallace, the Duke and Duchess of Norfolk, Mr. Noel Coward, The Master of Elphinstone, Mr. Peter Cazalet, Lord Salisbury, Mr. Peter Ustinov, The Hon. Mrs. Wills and Norman Hackforth.

How to please such a cosmopolitan party?

The fact is that, on special occasions, most women feel the need to provide something special. It makes them less anxious somehow.

So it was with royalty. I would make a list of initial suggestions, and the Queen or Queen Mother would select the final dishes very carefully.

We had some very simple menus at Clarence House, but also some very grand ones. I enjoyed doing both.

The following are a mixture of both. Some simple, some complicated. I will warn you about the complicated ones. However, if you are looking for a contract, prestige, a man or just a challenge, you will not be deterred.

Oeuf Cocotte aux tomates
Chicken Americane

Bouchèes Champignon
Beans and Crisp Potatoes
Salad
Banana Caramel

This is a fairly simple dinner for four people. Not obviously grand, but delights with small surprises.

OEUFS EN COCOTTE AUX TOMATES

4 *eggs*
2 *tomatoes*
¼ *pint of double cream*

½ *cup of grated parmesan*
cheese
seasoning

Skin the tomatoes. A quick way of doing this is to hold them over a low flame on a fork. Grease the china cocotte dishes with butter and add slices of seasoned tomatoes. Slide a whole raw egg into each dish. Cover each egg with a spoonful of double cream and sprinkle some grated cheese on top. Put them under the grill to brown. When golden brown, place them in a moderate oven for five minutes so that the eggs are almost set but still wobbly.

CHICKEN AMERICAINE

2 *spring chickens weighing*
   about 18 *to* 20 *ozs*
2 *beaten eggs*
seasoning

garlic salt
breadcrumbs
½ *lb butter*
flour

Dislocate both the spring chickens into four pieces. Remove the skin, then the bones by cutting down the middle of each joint. Keep the bones for stock. Season the chicken joints with pepper, salt and a little garlic salt. Flour, egg and breadcrumb the joints and fry gently in butter until golden brown. Place on a buttered tin and put in a moderate oven for fifteen minutes to finish.

BOUCHÉES CHAMPIGNON

4 *vol au vont cases (from the baker)*
½ *lb mushrooms*
2 *cups of milk*

½ *tablespoon flour*
nut of butter
pinch of sugar
pepper and salt

Slice the mushrooms, pour one and a half cups of milk over them in a saucepan, bring to the boil, season and simmer for two to three minutes. Dilute the flour with half a cup of milk, add to the mushrooms and cook slowly for ten minutes. Remove from the heat and add the butter and sugar. Fill the vol au vont cases with this mixture.

Serve the chicken in a dish with the mushroom bouchees, beans, fresh or frozen, some thinly cut fried potatoes, and salad according to season.

BANANA CARAMEL

1 *banana to each person*
¼ *lb butter*
2 *tablespoons of single cream*

1 *teaspoon of orange curaco or*
½ *teaspoon vanilla essence*
2 *tablespoons of golden syrup*

Mash the bananas and fry in butter. Remove, cool, and add the orange curaco or vanilla and the cream. Fill some wide topped glasses with this mixture.

To make the caramel topping heat the golden syrup in a saucepan and boil until brown. Pour on to a buttered tin and spread thinly. When cold, chip and sprinkle onto the banana mixture.

The following is the menu to produce only when there is a

lot at stake, because, frankly, it will take you about all day. It is not that any of the courses are particularly complicated, but there is quite a lot of detail in the preparation, and as all the dishes are rather subtle in flavour, any skimping or hurrying will render them pointless. I cannot remember the particular occasion on which I produced this menu at Clarence House, but I do recall that the Queen, like most people, was a little doubtful about the venison. All that I can say about this recipe for venison is that it is different and that I received a personal thank you and further requests for it.

In preparing this menu I would be inclined to make the consommé the day before. Then get the ice cream off first, then the venison, leaving the final cooking of the turbot until last. The recipe serve 8.

Consomme Julienne
Turbot Fritters Tartare Sauce
Braised Venison
Boiled Potatoes, Peas and Beans
Crème Marron

CONSOMMÉ JULIENNE

1 *lb shin of beef*	4 *pints of cold water*
1 *lb shin of veal*	1 *teaspoon of sugar*
1 *carrot*	1 *dessertspoon of salt*
1 *onion*	1 *clove*
1 *celery stalk*	*carrot, parsnip and parsley for*
10 *white peppercorns*	*garnish*

Cut the meat into small pieces and put in the water. Heat slowly, gradually bringing to the boil. Remove scum and add the vegetables to the meat. Add the salt, peppercorns, sugar

7

and clove and simmer over a low heat for three hours or more. Boil the carrot and parsnip garnish for a couple of minutes and cut into thin strips. Strain the soup and let it cool. Skim off fat when cold. Strain through muslin, save two tablespoons of the meat, cut into small pieces and put back into the soup. Garnish with the thinly cut vegetables and serve very hot with cheese straws or croutons.

TURBOT FRITTERS

2 *lbs of filleted turbot*   4½ *ozs of flour*
salt and pepper   6 *ozs of milk*
lemon   1 *tablespoon of nut oil*
2 *eggs*

Wash the fish and dry thoroughly. Cut up into fingers, season with pepper and salt and a squeeze of lemon. Sprinkle with flour.

To make the batter: beat about threequarters of the milk into the flour, beat in the eggs, then the oil. Continue beating until smooth.

Dip the fingers into the batter and fry in deep oil until golden brown. Serve with Tartare sauce (recipe see page 20).

BRAISED VENISON

4 *lbs of fillet of venison*   1 *oz of butter*
¾ *lb of fat larding bacon*   2 *tablespoons of flour*
2 *tablespoons of red currant*   1 *carrot*
   jelly   1 *onion*
1 *wineglass of rather vinegary*   1 *pint of stock or water*
   burgundy   *pepper, salt, garlic salt.*
½ *teacup of cream*

Wrap the larding bacon round the fillets of venison. Melt the butter in a saucepan and brown the meat. Cut up the carrot and onion and put in the pan with the stock or water. Add the pepper, salt and garlic salt and braise in a low oven for two hours. Remove the meat and vegetables from the pan and skim off the fat. Mix the flour with some water and stir into the gravy. Let it boil on top of the stove for a few minutes to reduce the gravy. Strain into another saucepan and add the red currant jelly and more stock if necessary. Add the wine and simmer for three minutes. Remove from heat. Dish up the venison and spoon a little of the sauce over it. Last of all stir in the cream and serve the rest of the sauce separately.

Only the plainest of vegetables, such as small boiled potatoes, peas or beans are necessary with this dish.

CRÈME MARRON

1 *pint of double cream*
½ *pint of vanilla ice cream (optional)*
1 *lb of chestnuts*
¼ *lb of sugar*

2 *ozs of cold butter*
a couple of drops of vanilla essence or maraschino to taste
1 *orange*

Peel the chestnuts and boil in a quarter of a pint of water until dry. Put the chestnuts through a metal sieve, add the butter and sugar and mix to a smooth cream. Put the cream in a forcing bag and pipe the mixture round and round the border of a silver dish. Mix the whipped cream with the vanilla ice cream and add the essence or maraschino, sweeten if necessary. Pile into the centre of the dish. If dispensing with the ice cream, merely mix the flavouring into the double cream. Decorate with pipped, peeled and sweetened orange slices.

This is a luncheon menu, which if I may say so, is *dis-*

creetly good and well balanced. There are several rather distinctive touches which will show imagination but not flamboyance. A splendid menu for in-laws or deals.

Grilled Ugly Fruit
Tournedos Sauté
Pomme Frites, Petit Pois, Salade
Pineapple Cake

GRILLED UGLY FRUIT

Half an Ugly fruit to each person
sugar

Cut and pip the Ugly fruit like a grapefruit. Cover with caster sugar and grill until brown. Serve hot.

TOURNEDOS SAUTÉ

1 tournedos steak to each person
2 ozs butter
1 tablespoon Madeira wine
½ lb ox kidney

½ pint stock
1 teaspoon flour
1 oz butter to each steak and 1 oz over

Fry tournedos in butter for five minutes on each side. Remove from pan and keep hot though not cooking. Melt butter in a saucepan, work in the flour until brown, stir in the stock and the chopped kidney. Cook for fifteen minutes and add the Madeira. Serve the tournedos with the sauce poured over them.

Nothing better with it than chipped potatoes, peas and green salad.

PINEAPPLE CAKE

1 fresh pineapple or one large tin
8 ozs butter
8 ozs sugar
6 ozs plain flour

1 heaped teaspoon baking powder
2 ozs cornflour
3 eggs

Pulp the fresh or tinned pineapple, by grating or putting in a mixer and add sugar to taste. Put in a greased fireproof dish and keep warm. Cream together the butter, sugar, eggs, flour and baking powder. Put the cake mixture on top of the pineapple pulp and bake in a moderate oven for three-quarters of an hour. Loosen carefully. Turn out and serve with cream.

Here is a menu for which I have a particular affection. Nearly all the ingredients are good, unpretentious and valuable. In that way it is a simple menu. But success depends on a certain amount of planning ahead. The pudding can be done ahead, but the soup should be served straight away. If you are cook-hostess, the veal will keep while the other courses are being served but ideally, the fish should be served at the last minute.

This dinner party is for six.

Cockie Leekie soup
Sole à la sauce rémoulade
Veal cutlets farcie
Cucumber Salad and Small Boiled Potatoes
Orange Fromage

COCKIE LEEKIE SOUP

2 *pints of veal bone stock*
2 *large potatoes*
2 *leeks*
pinch of sugar
2 *eggs*
$\frac{1}{4}$ *pint single cream*
$\frac{1}{2}$ *cup of grated gruyere cheese*
knob of butter
seasoning

Peel and cube the potatoes, skin the leeks and cut the white part into rings. Put the vegetables into the stock and cook until soft, add seasoning and sugar. Whip the eggs and cream in a basin. Take the vegetables out of the stock, remove from heat and thicken with the beaten eggs and cream. Add the butter and last thing, the cheese. Keep hot, but do not allow to cook as otherwise the soup will curdle.

The making of this soup merits your closest attention.

SOLE À LA SAUCE RÉMOULADE

2 *filleted Dover soles*
1 *cup of good stock*
1 *lb of potatoes, mashed and creamed*
seasoning

½ *pint of shrimps and parsley for decoration*
sauce rémoulade (recipe see page 22)

Rinse fillets and dry well. Season and place in a tin with the stock. Cover with greaseproof paper and poach in a moderate oven for fifteen minutes. Border a nice dish with the creamed potatoes, drain the fish and arrange in the middle. Coat with the sauce rémoulade and decorate with shrimps and parsley.

VEAL CUTLETS FARCIE

2 *lbs of veal from the leg*
1 *teacup of fresh breadcrumbs*
2 *eggs*
½ *cup of warm milk*

½ *teaspoon of sugar*
pepper, salt, pinch of nutmeg
½ *cup of white wine*
butter

Use the veal bone for stock and cut the meat from the leg. Put the meat twice through the mincer on a medium plate. Mix the breadcrumbs with the milk and work it into the mince meat. Add the beaten eggs, seasoning, sugar and nutmeg. Mix well and mould into cutlets. Fry in butter on both sides for ten minutes. Add some more butter to the frying pan if necessary and pour in some stock and the wine; simmer fast to reduce the quantity and pour some onto the cutlets. Serve the rest separately.

Dish up on a plate bordered with plain boiled rice and heaped in the centre, button mushrooms sautéd in butter. Instead of a cooked vegetable, try cucumber salad (method page 84).

ORANGE FROMAGE

6 *small juicy oranges*
3 *tablespoons of sugar*
1 *pint of gelatine or a block of*
  orange jelly

½ *lb of cream cheese*
roasted flaked almonds
1 *pint of water*

Decapitate the oranges and remove pips and fibrous centre, but otherwise leave whole. Put the oranges in a saucepan of water, add the sugar and cook gently until soft. Cool in the syrup. Either make a jelly with the syrup and gelatine or use a proprietary make of orange jelly, leaving it to set in a dish large enough to take the oranges. Place the oranges in a dish and pour in the jelly just before setting point. Pipe the cream cheese into the oranges and spoon over some of the jelly to make a glaze. Decorate with the almonds.

Serve very cold.

Dinner at eight . . . and you could set your clock by the Queen's appearance at the dinner table with her guests. This punctuality, I am sure is dictated by a natural consideration for the people who work for her. Dinner at eight meant that on a good day I could be finished in the kitchen by 10 p.m. I always saw the dinner through down to the serving of the coffee, although of course I did not have to wash up. After this I went to my room and wrote out the menus for the following day. Oddly enough that was my greatest headache.

The menus had to be in French and being no scholar of languages I used to struggle for hours with the language of haute cuisine. Eventually I found a wonderful, but very expensive, book which contained all the terms I needed, though I was still conscious of the odd mistake.

However, the Queen, who speaks excellent French, was very kind about this and tactfully ignored any errors.

When you are cooking for royalty, of course, every day is in a sense a special occasion. Two very special guests at Clarence House before Princess Elizabeth became Queen were her mother and father. On the occasions of their visits, the menu was a matter of detailed selection.

The following is a right royal menu, in that all the ingredients are of the very best. The preparation is a matter of love, care and patience, and in all fairness I will say that I have never attempted this menu as a cook-hostess. If you are to cook and to appear at your own dinner table, you will need help. The soup, pudding and foie gras can be forwarded but the fish and chicken courses must have close attention.

Consomme à la Charlotte

Turbot à la Crème Citron

Filet de Volaille à la Princesse

aux Pointes d'Asperges

Sauce Champignons

Salade Française

Parfait Ananas Royale

Petits fours

Fois Gras Chantilly Strasbourg

Maçedoine Fruits

CONSOMMÉ À LA CHARLOTTE

1 *lb of shin of beef*
1 *lb of shin of veal*
1 *carrot*
1 *onion*
1 *stick of celery*
10 *whole white peppercorns*
1 *clove*

1 *teaspoon of sugar*
1 *glass of medium sweet white wine*
4 *pints of water*
1 *lb of whole roasted walnuts*
½ *lb of muscatel grapes*

Make a clear consommé according to the method given for Consommé Julienne (see page 97) and remove all the vegetables. Allow to cool, skim off fat and strain through a muslin cloth. Then add the wine and serve very hot with the scraped walnuts and the pipped and skinned grapes floated in each dish.

This soup improves if kept overnight at the cooling stage.

I had the nerve to call this Consommé 'Charlotte' after one of my own names, as this soup is very much my own creation.

TURBOT À LA CRÈME CITRON

4 *fillets of turbot*
1 *glass of white wine*
1 *glass of fish stock*

1 *lemon*
parsley

Poach the fillets in wine and stock in a moderate oven for fifteen minutes. Remove the fish from the juice. Dish up and cover with crème citron (recipe page 24). Decorate with parsley and thinly sliced lemon.

FILETS DE VOLAILLE À LA PRINCESSE

Breasts of chicken (1 *to each person and some over*)
1 *lb of veal*
1 *lb of gammon*
½ *cup of cream*

butter for cooking
2 *oranges and watercress for decoration*
seasoning

Make a forcemeat by mincing the veal and gammon together and mixing with the cream. Season. Skin the breasts of chicken, put a tablespoon of forcemeat on each piece of chicken and fry gently in butter until golden brown. Then place in a medium oven and cook for ten minutes.

SAUCE CHAMPIGNONS

1 *cup of chicken stock*
1 *dessertspoon of flour*
½ *pint of milk*
1 *tablespoon of butter*
½ *teaspoon of sugar*
seasoning
½ *lb of mushrooms*

Slice the mushrooms and boil them for two minutes in the milk. Make a sauce from the chicken stock thickened with flour. Add the mushrooms, seasoning and sugar and, lastly, the cold butter.

Dish up the chicken fillets and glaze them with some of their own juice. Plunge the oranges into boiling water, quarter, remove pips but leave the skins. Decorate the chicken fillets with the orange quarters and watercress.

Serve the sauce champignons and asparagus tips separately.

SALADE FRANÇAISE

Fresh lettuce hearts in French dressing.
(*For my own salad dressing see page* 83.)

PARFAIT ANANAS ROYALE

ice cream mixture (*for recipe see page* 64)
1 *pineapple or a large tin of pineapple rings*
6 *ozs caster sugar*

Roughly grate half the pineapple and add to the ice cream

mixture with a little sugar. Put the mixture in a tin or mould and freeze for three hours. Make some caramel by placing the sugar in a heavy saucepan over a gentle heat and dissolving slowly without stirring. Boil steadily to a rich brown and pour into a greased tin. Allow to cool. Turn the parfait out on to a silver or crystal dish and decorate with thinly sliced pineapple rings. Sprinkle the crunched caramel artistically.

Serve with petit fours.

FOIE GRAS CHANTILLY STRASBOURG

½ *lb of paté de foie gras*
¼ *pint of whipped cream*
½ *pint of Aspic jelly (set)*
lettuce

fresh fruit salad made from slices of peeled and pipped grapefruit, pear, apple and peach soaked in grapefruit juice to preserve the colour

Sieve the foie gras and mix it with the whipped cream. Have ready two tablespoons in hot water and scoop the foie gras into a silver dish. This will give the impression of eggs in a basket. Sprinkle the chopped aspic round the foie gras and pile the fruit on lettuce leaves in the same dish.

Serve with Melba toast.

And the best of British luck!

THE LAST WORD

THE LAST WORD

Now at sixty-six I spend a good deal of my time in the garden—a return to that most fulfilling of hobbies which I first learned to enjoy all those years ago in Sweden.

But even now I get offers to cook for well-known people who like my sort of food; and off I go for a few days or weeks. And I still find the challenge of providing good food for people who appreciate it an irresistible stimulus.

I started cooking because I liked it and found it was a way in which I could please people and add to their well-being, I have tried never to lose sight of this simple theme, and all the nice, exciting things that have happened to me in my life, have sprung from this philosophy. If I had followed a different course, I could have been richer, but not, I believe, so happy.

One more thing I should like to point out. All the best things that happened to me occurred late in life. I married late, I reached the peak of my career when I was over fifty. Even now I have discovered a new and useful phase in my life. I do not believe that there is ever a time in a woman's life when she need feel bored or useless.

And the root of all this happiness? The humble art of cooking.